CW01033064

WATER AT WOI

RIVERS (pp. 1-29)

The Davisian model is not mentioned. It seems more helpful for work on a continental scale (as U.S.A.) than for Britain. However pp. 17-29 could be used in that context if a teacher wished.

Down the stream (pp. 1-6)

pp. 2-5
The simple activities using plastic guttering can be carried out as group work or as a class demonstration. They demonstrate basic river-flow concepts.

p. 6
Samples of each kind of rock, and a boulder weighing about 7 kg would be useful aids. The large boulders were transported during flood or bank-full discharge conditions (or possibly during wetter climatic phases with greater average discharge).

Rivers and drainage (pp. 7-10)

p. 7
The text is written so that the probable findings from the sand-tray activities are mentioned afterwards for students who do not do the practical work. The authors believe that the practical (or demonstration) work is invaluable, but appreciate that such activities are not always possible.

pp. 8-10
These pages need careful reading and should be slowly worked through. It is important to make sure the right figure is referred to each time. Each question is simple in itself, but if the reading or work is hurried the separate steps could become confused.

p. 9
Fig. 17 - Basin P: (ii) and (iv). Basin Q: (i) and (iii). Basin P is typical of chalk lands.
Fig. 19 is held back onto p. 9 for the full colour.

p. 10
Fig. 20 - about 6 times as much water can be expected to flow through B (6 times the area drained).
Fig. 21 - the peat holds water, so the water drains off slowly.
Fig. 19 shows little or no peat and steep slope, so the water drains off quickly. The area with

fast drainage on Fig. 20 is to the South of the mainstream (the River Noe), where there is a high density of streams, just below the viewpoint for Fig. 18 (but visible on Fig. 19).

Although there are a lot of river channels to the South of the River Noe their discharge would be low after 5 days without rain, since there is little peat to hold water in their small catchment area.

How streams carve the land (pp. 11-20)

p. 12
Fig. 26 - the greater cross-sectional area of the stream at A allows the same volume of water to pass in a second even though the speed of the current is slower.

p. 14
Fig. 31 - similar sketches could be traced and labelled from other photographs later in the text.

p. 16
Discharge for wavelength 35 metres would be about 0.35 m^3/s. Bank-full discharge of 0.35 m^3/s would need 5 times the surveyed discharge, and the river 25 cm deep, which approximately fits the section Fig. 33 shown in (b).

p. 18
Fig. 41 - this diagram is small, but it could be used to trace an overhead projector transparency for classroom use.

pp. 19-20
Fig. 32 - the block diagrams are drawn with a great vertical exaggeration (x 10 approximately).

Moving mountains (pp. 21-29)

p. 23
First line - 150 000 m^3 'of material' in one night!
Fig. 48 - the material was deposited as shingle and rock, and probably has helped to build up the 'sand ridge'.

p. 26
Fig. 53 - same key as Fig. 51.

p. 28
Fig. 56 - X : weir and locks; Y : maintained new channel to link the River Avon to the River Severn; the main stream of the River Avon previously followed the course marked as 'Old Avon'.

p. 29
Fig. 60 - County and parish boundary, stream courses, tree lines, and field boundaries suggest earlier river course. The river course is straightened in the northern part of the map, and held by earth banks.

SEAS AND SEA-SHORES (pp. 30-37)

p. 31
Fig. 63 - could be replaced by the current year's
times and heights.

p. 32
Fig. 64 - shows tidal change and waves.

p. 33
Fig. 67(a) is further out from the line of the
coast, is only just above the L.W. mark, spends
less time above the water-mark each day, and is
less sheltered from the open sea.

p. 34
Line 13 - for Fig. 47 read Fig. 70.

p. 36
Fig. 74 - the river current stops material moving
past the estuary along the coast by longshore
drift, especially at low tide. Storm waves and
wind build up material above the H.W. mark. A lot
of the material brought down by the river is
deposited in the estuary behind the spit.

WHEN THE WATERS FREEZE (pp. 37-42)

Discussion by class groups or pairs of each point
in the argument between Dr Flood and Professor
Overall would be very useful.

p. 41
The scratches in Anglesey were formed by Irish Sea
Ice. The Snowdonia Ice Sheet was much more
localised.

Further study 1: MORE ICE AGE LANDSCAPES
(pp. 43-44)

A short study, but important since so much
British landscape was moulded in periglacial
conditions.

Further study 2: LANDS WITHOUT WATER
(pp. 45-47)

p. 45
Fig. 2.3 - the largest stones are about 50 cm
across.

p. 47
Fig. 2.6 - large scale slumping and 'river-
channels' are clearly visible through a hand lens.
The large crater is probably about 15 km across.

Further study 6: MEASURING RIVERS
(pp. 55-57)

This section suggests fieldwork measurements that
can be taken on small rivers using very basic
cheap equipment.
These fieldwork measurements should be made in the
context of some planned fieldwork investigation,
possibly framed around hypotheses or questions
derived from the section on Rivers, especially
pp. 1-16.   For example:

> 'As the area drained by a river
> increases, its discharge
> increases.'

> 'The speed of the main current
> through a rapids section is
> always faster than through a
> pool section.'

> 'Water on the inside of bend in
> a pool section is almost still.'

> 'The speed of the current
> increases when the cross-
> sectional area of the stream
> gets less.'

There are of course many other investigations that
can be linked to these particular stream flow
measurements: these could involve the gradient of
the water surface, long profiles, stream-bed
material and so on.

p. 57
The discharge of very small streams can be
measured using a calibrated container (plastic
ice-cream box [2 litres], or bucket). A small
waterfall can be 'modified' to make the equivalent
of a V-notched weir. The time taken to fill the
container, or the volume of water flowing into it
in a given time, can be measured. 1 litre per
second (1 l/s) = 0.001 m^3/s.
The drawings for Figs. 6.5 and 6.7 are artist's
representations.   The graph paper does not match
the results in the text and in the table.
The cross sections as they appear in Figs. 6.5 and
6.7 are not identical. The table of results from
the cross section as it appears in Fig. 6.7 would
be:-

Section	Speed m/s	Cross-section area (squares x 0.01)m^2	Discharge m^3/s
A	0.33	6 x 0.01 = 0.06	0.020
B	0.45	10 x 0.01 = 0.10	0.045
C	0.56	44 x 0.01 = 0.44	0.246
D	0.42	10 x 0.01 = 0.10	0.042
Total for river		0.70	0.353

(One square on the graph paper represents
0.1 m x 0.1 m = 0.01 m^2.)

The simple discharge measurement using the average
speed of 0.50 m/s would be 0.70 m^2 x 0.50 =
0.35 m^3/s for the cross section drawn in Fig. 6.7.

Further study 7: SAND-TRAY ACTIVITIES
(pp. 58-64)

These activities seem often to lift the veil of
mystery, and the 'concrete' succeeds where word
and picture don't. They are a substitute for
frequent fieldwork which may not be possible. The
instructions are for activities with small amounts
of cheap equipment, which can be set up in any
classroom. A bucket of water, occasionally
refilled, and a bucket for 'slops' will suffice if
a room has no taps and sink.

A few small points not emphasised in the text:
boxes can have drain holes or be 'baled' with
plastic cartons. The sand must be damp for any
river or coastal landscape activities. The box
must be tilted for any river work - a slope in the
sand is not adequate. The sand will take a few
minutes to drain off before a second activity can
be attempted in the same tray.

Instructions should emphasise the importance of a
gentle flow (a trickle) for the start of any river
simulations.

p. 62
Activity S8 is the most difficult because the sand
can become saturated too quickly.

AIR AND EARTH

THE WEATHER (pp. 3-16)

The sections on weather do not introduce weather
instruments, nor observation and recording. It is
assumed that these topics will have been part of
the earlier work. This section concentrates on
the difficult concept of atmospheric pressure and
its effect on the weather.

What is it like today? (pp. 3-6)

pp. 3-4
'Revision' of elementary ideas and relating
objective weather records to experience.

pp. 5-6
Introducing pressure and its variation with
altitude. Page 6 could be linked to biological
experiments on students' own lung capacity,
number of breaths etc.

High or low? (pp. 7-16)

pp. 7-10
The small experiments can be done as
demonstrations, and, though there must be problems
of transfer from this scale to that of 'real'
weather, it is important to start from some
concrete examples.

p. 9
The cloud pictures are also on the back cover in
colour.

p. 11
1 - (c), 2 - (a), 3 - (b), 4 - (d).

pp. 12-13
The skill of interpreting isobars may need
practice - expect to use a rubber!

pp. 14-15
There are some doubts about the accuracy of the
analogy in *Activity 3* - but it seems to make the
theory more understandable.

WEATHER ON THE MOVE (pp. 17-27)

This section develops through discussion of the
weather associated with fronts to an understanding of weather maps like those presented on TV.
The traditional 'frontal model' is used with a
little additional information (e.g. Fig. 38),

since this still seems to present an accurate
enough generalisation for this level of work.

When warm and cold air meet (pp. 17-23)

p. 17
Satellite photos and up-to-date information are
available free in *Mariners Weather Log*, NOAA,
Environmental Data Service, D762, Page Building 1,
Room 400, Washington D.C. 20235, U.S.A.

p. 19
Fig. 35 is not a complete success - the cloud
cover is meant to be a flat layer over the
British Isles. Its aim is in particular to show
the true vertical scale of cloud cover, and
rectify the false impression that can be given by
diagrams like Fig. 34.

p. 21
The clouds at the centre of the photo (Fig. 32)
spiral up, but the fronts on the map (Fig. 39) are
only marked where they touch the ground.

Rainfall (pp.23-24)

Further study 1: TRACKS AND RAIN
(p. 48)

pursues this topic in more detail.

WEATHER ATTACKS (pp. 28-40)

This section is about the formation and
characteristics of soils. The approach is through
practical work. Nearly all the soil activities
can be done without much equipment on desks or
tables covered with newspapers.

Breaking up rocks (pp. 28-30)

pp. 28, 29
The activities can be demonstrations and results
shown 'next lesson'.

Soil (pp. 30-33)

p. 30
It is important in *Activity 8* to break the soil up
very finely, and to put the jar down quickly and
level after shaking.

p. 33
Profile (*b*) top to bottom A-B-C.
Profile (*c*) top to bottom A-C-C.

It would be useful to dig a profile pit, or use a
river bank or a roadside cutting, to show a soil
profile 'in situ' during fieldwork.

What happens in the soil? (pp. 35-40)

p. 35
The soil drainage activity needs some care - the
soil should be as near to its natural condition as
possible. Ideally the tin should be pressed into
the soil outside to collect a sample. Otherwise
the soil must be well broken first, then packed
down a little.

p. 37
Activity 13 uses the simplest method for measuring
the pH number of a soil. More accurate measurements can be made using a Soil Test Kit (Universal
or Soil Indicator liquid, distilled water, barium
sulphate, glass tube with 2 corks, soil indicator
colour chart).

p. 40
Gardens, left to right - clay; chalk; sand.
A useful teacher's book on soil is *The Soil : An
Introduction to Soil Study in Britain* by
F.M. Courtney and S.T. Trudgill (Edward Arnold)
1976.

LIFE IN THE AIR AND EARTH (pp. 41-47)

pp. 42-44
Fig. 74 runs over 3 **pages**.

p. 43
This page needs slow careful study. The breaks in
the vertical scale of Fig. 76 make it impossible
to estimate the rainfall value for the medians.
They can however be looked up on Fig. 75.

Narrow rings median 1896 - 630 mm.
Wide rings median 1901 - 730 mm.

Fig. 77 - 1890 and 1891 both years with wide rings
but low total rainfall. However in both cases the
shortage was not during the main summer growing
season.

p. 44
Apparently the data in Fig. 78 **do not** help to
explain the growth (the reverse actually!).

p. 45
Fig. 81   (a) - D; (b) - A; (c) - B; (d) - C.

Further study 1: TRACKS AND RAIN (pp. 48-52)

p. 50
Fig. 1.5

Prestwick L1 - 1.5 mm, L2 - 10.5 mm, L3 - 0 mm.
Gatwick   L1 - 10 mm, L2 - 9 mm, L3 - 16 mm.

Refer to Fig. 1.1 for locations of Prestwick and
Gatwick.

p. 52
Fourth reason - altitude and aspect.

Further study 2: A WET WEEKEND
(pp. 53-55)

p. 53
The river was diverted so that the field could be used for games.

p. 54
The anticyclone blocked the depression and it was virtually stationary.

p. 55
The sequence of maps is left to right top row then left to right bottom row. Fig. 2.5 - Cold front rainfall: 11 p.m. (2300) Friday through to 6 a.m. (0600) Saturday, by which time the weather map shows the cold front (at ground level) almost at Bournville.

Little depression rainfall: 10 p.m. (2200) Saturday to 1 a.m. (0100) Sunday. It is hard to say what caused the showers 1600 - 1800 hours Saturday.

Further study 3:
THE JET STREAM AND BLOCKING PATTERNS
(pp. 56-59)

The positions of the jet stream were interpreted from the 500 mb surface in the atmosphere, shown on daily weather maps in the *European Meteorological Bulletin*, published in Offenbach, West Germany.

p. 57
(i) Path X guides depression across Britain.
(ii) Path Y to the north.
(iii) Path Z to the south.

  (i) X - alternating air masses
 (ii) Y - warm only
(iii) Z - cool only

August 1976 - Y.

pp. 58, 59
L1 moved off on 2nd March.

- jet stream in southern position, 2nd, 3rd, 4th March guided it along English Channel.

L2 moved off on 5th March.
- jet stream on northerly route 5th and 6th guided it north.

L3 - 8th March - jet stream back on southerly track.

Further study 5: MAKE YOUR OWN SOIL MAP
(pp. 61-63)

p. 62
Fig. 5.5 - if possible demonstrate the use of a soil auger.

Further study 6: SOIL EROSION
(pp. 64-67)

p. 64
Fig. 6.1 The photos show (left to right, top to bottom) sheet erosion by water; gulley erosion by water; wind erosion.

p. 65
Sand tray activities - see Teachers' Notes for *Water at Work*.

pp. 66-67
Farm 1 Shelter belts, strip cropping.
Farm 2 Terracing, contour ploughing, strip cropping.
Farm 3 Afforestation of steep slopes above farm.

p. 67
Fig. 6.4 Photos show (left to right, top to bottom): strip cropping and contour ploughing; terracing; shelter belts; afforestation of steep slopes with conifers (background especially).

Further study 7: MAN-MADE PROBLEMS
(pp. 68-72)

pp. 71, 72
Activities - make sure there are algae in the pond water.

Further study 8:
PLANTS AND PLANT COMMUNITIES
(pp. 73-77)

p. 73
There are many suitable books for flower recognition in most libraries. The authors found *The Pocket Encyclopaedia of Wild Flowers in Colour*, by M. Skythe Christiansen (Blandford Press Ltd., 1974) useful, even though it was originally published in Denmark.

Further study 9: IS THE CLIMATE CHANGING?
(pp. 78-80)

This further study could not be **def**initive, but
hopes to stimulate interest. Nigel Calder's
The Weather Machine and the Threat of Ice (BBC,
1974), is an interesting source book.

ROCKS AND EARTH HISTORY

Using the book

This book in the *Study the Earth* series is meant
to be an interesting and stimulating introduction
to the fundamentals of geology. Along with the
fourth book in the series, *Useful Materials from
the Earth*, it could form the basis of the first
year or so of a two-year course in geology leading
to a CSE or GCE examination. Used more selectively,
it could provide material for the geological
component of a core science course for 11 - 16
pupils. The approach is based on practical
activities and fieldwork observations through case
studies, and the overriding aim is to guide pupils
into providing their own interpretations of a wide
range of geological phenomena. Teachers will
readily recognize that the book cannot be regarded
as a completely comprehensive CSE or GCE Geology
course, and the more formal and more advanced work
that comes later on would have to be provided by a
book such as Michael Bradshaw's *The Earth : Past,
Present and Future* (Hodder and Stoughton, 1980).

The Association of Teachers of Geology

There are several important benefits of joining
this Association, not least the regular receipt of
the journal, *Geology Teaching*. References to this
are given in the notes that follow.

Fieldwork

Fieldwork exercises should be an integral part of
any geology course. All geology teachers should
have copies of: *A Code for Geological Field Work*
(available as a leaflet from The Geologists'
Association of London) and *The Fieldwork Code of
the National Association of Field Study Officers*
(reproduced in *Geology Teaching* (1980) 5, 2)

Audio-visual aids

Geology courses can be supported by a range of
audio-visual aids. Filmstrips and slides are
available from a number of educational suppliers
and 16 mm films can be obtained on free loan from
the major oil companies. The BBC TV series *On the
Rocks* (with the accompanying book) is an excellent
production and is pitched at about the right level
so long as it is used selectively.

DIFFERENT KINDS OF HISTORY (pp. 1-2)

The 'continents adrift' cartoon is based on an idea by J. C. Holden in *Sea Frontiers* (R.S. Dietz, 1967).

Two concepts mentioned in this section are fundamental to an understanding of geology; geological history as a sequence of events through geological time, and the use of observations on present-day processes as a means of unravelling this history from the evidence in the rocks.

DIFFERENT KINDS OF ROCKS (pp. 2-14)

Rocks in layers (pp. 2-7)

pp. 2-4
The fieldwork case study should be seen as an introduction to pupils' own fieldwork and not as a replacement for it. An exposure of layered sedimentary rocks local to the school (if possible) should be found where pupils can make their own measurements. The essentials for this kind of work are a notebook, pencil and rubber, a tape measure, a compass (calibrated in degrees from 0 to 360°) and a clinometer.
Each dip should be expressed as an *angle* in degrees to the horizontal (as measured by the clinometer) and as a *direction* (as measured by the compass). The clinometer should be moved around the chosen bedding plane until it is placed in the position giving the maximum angle. It should then be kept in this position so that a compass can be used to determine the direction of dip. This exercise emphasizes that the dip of layered rocks may be 'apparent' (less than the maximum) or 'real' (the maximum).

When we look at a layered exposure, the dip we see will only be the 'real' one if the exposure runs exactly parallel to the direction of dip (i.e. at right angles to the strike). If the exposure runs at an angle to the direction of dip, then the 'apparent' dip will be at a lower angle than the 'real' dip. In the extreme case, the exposure might run at right angles to the direction of dip (i.e. along the strike) and then the layers will appear to be horizontal.

These considerations can be made clearer by using a model dipping strata made from layers of differently coloured plasticine and 'sliced' in several different directions. It is, in any case, worthwhile for pupils to make their own plasticine models based on their fieldwork exposure.

Clinometers

Several types are available commercially. One of the cheapest is the Burgess Powerline Level and Angle Indicator available from Lythe Minerals, 2 Wellsic Lane, Rothley, Leics. The details for constructing a home-made liquid-level clinometer are given in *Geology Teaching* (1980) *5*, 3.

Activity 1 Looking at a sandstone (p. 4)
Each pupil or group requires a piece of paper or a paper plate, a hand lens, some ordinary orange sand, and a small lump of easily crumbled sandstone (e.g. a Permo-Triassic sandstone or another of the Mesozoic sandstones).

Activity 2 Making layers of sand (p. 4)
Each pupil or group requires two large jam jars or gas jars, some ordinary orange sand and some sand of a different colour (e.g. silver sand), and access to a water supply.

Activity 3 Making graded layers of sediment (p. 5)
Each pupil or group requires a large jam jar or gas jar, some gravel, some coarse sand and some fine sand, and access to a water supply. Soil could be used instead of the suggested mixture since it usually contains a range of grain sizes.

Activity 4 Making 'rock' from sand (p. 6)
Each pupil or group requires a small plastic syringe with its nozzle cut off, a paper plate or tile, a plastic spoon, a plastic cup or beaker, a hand lens, petroleum jelly, some damp sand, some clay powder, and some Plaster of Paris.

This activity first appeared in the curriculum materials of the Australian Science Education Project.

The least easily crumbled 'rock' is made in (c) and the most easily crumbled one in (a). Real sandstones vary considerably in toughness depending on the degree of compaction and the degree of cementation. Younger sandstones tend to be more easily crumbled than older ones.

Thin sections of sandstones (Fig. 13) can be purchased from some of the suppliers of geological materials. Pupils should have the opportunity of looking at such a thin section under an ordinary microscope and sketching what they see.

Another kind of layering (pp. 8-9)

Making cross-bedding in sediments (Fig. 17). For this demonstration, the teacher requires a 1-metre length of P.V.C. guttering, a clamp and stand, a block of wood as a support, a glass trough, a siphon tube, a bucket, a plastic cup or beaker (or a direct supply of water from the tap), some soil (or powdered coal) and some sand (each handful should contain about 100 cm^3 of solid).

Water should be poured from the cup or beaker onto the guttering just behind the sand or soil, but not too quickly since the material may then be carried too far across the trough. Also, too much sludging of the sand or soil masses produces an erosional depression in the top of the 'delta'. Some of the excess water will have to be siphoned out of the trough towards the end of the experiment. The cross-bedding can be viewed through the trough.

A simpler experiment that simulates the settling of sand grains on the lee side of a sand ripple, a sand dune or a delta is to roll a sealed coffee jar containing some dry sand along a bench.

Rocks with crystals (pp. 9-13)

Where possible, pupils should visit a local exposure of an igneous rock and compare it with an exposure of a sedimentary rock. Specimens of a typical granite, such as Shap granite, should be available for examination under a hand lens, and a thin section for examination under an ordinary microscope would also be useful.

Activity 5 Sorting out the crystals in granite (p. 9)
The teacher requires a large hammer, a cloth, and a lump of granite. Each pupil or group requires a needle, a hand lens, a paper plate or tile, and some crushed granite. It is best for the teacher to carry out the breaking up of the granite prior to the lesson.

Activity 6 Making crystals from a melt (pp. 10-11)
Each pupil or group requires:
  (a) a bunsen burner, a tripod and gauze, a beaker, a test-tube, a dropper, a hand lens, microscope slides, one from a fridge and one kept at room temperature, some salol (phenyl salicylate) or naphthalene, and access to a water supply and a gas supply.
  (b) a bunsen burner, a test-tube and holder, a beaker, some crushed roll sulphur, and access to a water supply and a gas supply.

The results achieved in part (a) using salol are far better than those using naphthalene. The hot molten sulphur in part (b) should be treated carefully to avoid accidents. A sulphurous smell is inevitable in this activity and the room needs to be well-ventilated.

There is a lively account of the way a 'geological detective' investigating the origin of an igneous rock from the size of its crystals in *Geology Teaching* (1980) *5*, 3. It takes the form of an imaginary dialogue between Sherlock Holmes and Dr. Watson.

The lava in Fig. 24 is probably at a temperature of around 900°C. The columnar jointing in Fig. 29 is formed by regular shrinkage during the cooling of the basalt melt.

Finding the age of a rock (pp. 13-14)

This case study of a rock succession should, where possible, be supported by a local example in the field. This is an appropriate point at which to provide pupils with a simplified geological succession of the local area, and the geological time-scale (see back cover).

The theme of the relative ages of the rocks and the structures in a given area is a recurring one throughout the book. The ultimate aim is for pupils to be able to piece together the 'story' in the rocks from fieldwork evidence and from simplified geological maps and sections. In this book, the highest level of development for the theme is to be found in Further study 5: ROCK CYCLES IN THE PAST.

THE CHANGING EARTH (pp. 15-26)

What is inside the earth? (pp. 15-19)

p. 16
The average thickness of the oceanic crust is 5 kilometres and of the continental crust is 33 kilometres (Fig. 36). The thickness of the continental crust can be as high as 70 kilometres under mountains.

Activity 7 Finding the relative densities of two crustal rocks (p. 16)
Each pupil or group requires access to a top-pan balance and a water supply, a displacement can, a tripod, a measuring cylinder with a suitable maximum volume, and small lumps of granite and basalt.

The relative densities of granite and basalt are just under 3. Because the average relative densities of the crust and the mantle are less than the average relative density of the earth, the relative density of the core must be greater than 5.5 (Fig. 38). In fact, the relative density of the core probably ranges from 9.5 to at least 14.5.

The 'hot spots' inside the earth (p. 18) contain very small amounts of molten material dispersed among the crystals of solid rock. Volcanoes are formed when the overlying rocks develop a weakness and the pressure on the 'hot spots' is reduced. This allows much more rock to melt and the magma so formed moves up towards the surface. As it rises, it looses gases to the atmosphere. The teacher could simulate these effects by shaking a full bottle of fizzy drink and then quickly removing the top.

Earthquakes and mountains (pp. 20-26)

p. 21
The extracts in Figs. 48 and 49 give readings of about 3 and 10 or 11 respectively on the Modified Mercalli Scale (Fig. 46). The teacher may also like to mention a recent 'major' British earthquake which occurred just after Christmas 1979 and had its epicentre near Dumfries in southern Scotland. It gave a reading of 5 on the Modified

Mercalli Scale and this kind of reading is about as high as we get in Britain.

pp. 22-24
The match of the earthquake and volcanic zones in Figs. 50 and 51 is very good, especially if the submarine volcanoes along the mid-oceanic ridges are also taken into account (not shown on Fig. 51). These active zones are at plate margins, which may be _constructive_ if new crust is being formed (Figs. 52 and 54) or _destructive_ if old crust is being destroyed (Figs. 55 and 56). The calculation based on Fig. 54 shows that the opening of the North Atlantic began around 60 m.y. ago.

p. 25
Fig. 57 is based on an illustration on pp. 86-87 of Nigel Calder's _Restless Earth_ (BBC, 1972).

Activity 8 Squeezing plasticine into folds (p. 25)
Each pupil or group requires some plasticine in at least two different colours, two small blocks of wood, a knife and a suitable flat working surface.

Completing the rock cycle (p. 26)

Figs. 44 and 60 can be fitted together by merging the red arrow labelled _'New magma formed'_ (Fig. 44) with the red arrow to the left of _'METAMORPHIC ROCKS'_ (Fig. 60). The red arrows drawn across the earth's surface are the same in each diagram.

RECOGNIZING MINERALS AND ROCKS (pp. 27-36)

Making a collection of minerals and rocks

The main sources of specimens are as follows:
  1. The local area. All schools teaching geology should have a comprehensive local collection.
  2. Holiday areas (of both staff and pupils).
  3. Local authority resources.

Some schools may be lucky enough to be able to take advantage of a museum loan service. In some areas, an LEA adviser might be a further source at in-service courses in geology/earth science.

  4. Educational suppliers. This is the easiest way of obtaining already identified specimens of the main types of minerals and rocks. They can be bought as individual specimens or in boxed reference collections. Possible sources include the usual suppliers of school science equipment and also the following specialist suppliers:

Gregory, Bottley & Co., 30 Old Church Street, Chelsea, London. SW3 5BY

Lythe Minerals, 2 Wellsic Lane, Rothley, Leicestershire. LE7 7QB

R.F.D. Parkinson & Co. Ltd., Geologist, Doulting, Shepton Mallet, Somerset. BA4 4RF

Richard Tayler Minerals, Byways, Burstead Close, Cobham, Surrey.

The Geological Laboratories, Lower Branscombe House, Ebford, Topsham, Exeter. Devon. EX3 0RA

When obtaining specimens, it is important to bear in mind two kinds of uses for them. For reference, only a few good specimens of each type are required and these will be carefully handled from year to year. However, larger quantities of some of these minerals and rocks will be required for pupils' practical activities. These must be regarded as 'consumable' items which will need replacing regularly. It is obviously desirable not to have to purchase this kind of specimen, if at all possible.

Reference specimens should be kept in a compartmentalized box or in separate small card-board trays. Each tray should be numbered and labelled and each specimen should have a number written in black ink on a 'blob' of white enamel paint. A key to the collection should also be compiled.

Minerals (pp. 27-31)

Activity 9 Comparing two minerals (pp. 28,29)
Each pupil or group requires specimens of two common white or transparent minerals (e.g. quartz, calcite, barite, gypsum), a hand lens, a 10p coin, a penknife, a streak plate (the unglazed back of a glazed tile would do), a dropper and a bottle of dilute (0.5 M) hydrochloric acid, another tile (for the acid test), and the apparatus for _Activity 7_ (if the relative densities of the minerals are to be found).

Hardness 'pencils', each of a stated hardness number, can be purchased from suppliers of school science equipment.

p. 29
The demonstration shown in Fig. 63 is not as easy as it looks: some prior practice is strongly recommended.

Activity 10 Using a flowchart to identify some minerals (p. 30)
Each pupil or group requires several unlabelled mineral specimens (selected from those in Fig. 66), and the apparatus and materials listed for _Activity 9_. Teachers and pupils may also wish to consult a standard reference book on minerals as well as using Figs. 66 and 67.

Rocks (pp. 32-36)

Activity 11 Comparing two rocks (pp. 32-33)
Each pupil or group requires specimens of two
common rocks (preferably one made from grains and
one from crystals), a hand lens; a knife, access to
a cloth, a hammer and a suitable surface (for the
procedure shown in Fig. 69); a dropper and a bottle
of dilute (0.5 M) hydrochloric acid, another tile
(for the acid test), and the apparatus for
Activity 7 (if the relative densities of the rocks
are to be found).

The distinction between a rock made from grains and
one made from crystals is fundamental and yet, in
practice, it is often difficult to make. It would
be useful at this stage for pupils to do some work
on thin sections of rocks, not, of course, going as
far as mineral identification under polarized light.
The aim would simply be to use an ordinary microscope to show the essential difference between a
granular rock and a crystalline rock.

*Activity 12 Using a flowchart and some keys to
identify some rocks* (pp. 35, 36)
Each pupil or group requires several unlabelled
rock specimens (selected from those in Figs. 72-76),
and the apparatus and materials listed for
Activity 11.

LIFE IN THE PAST (pp. 37-46)

Making a collection of fossils

The main sources of fossils are the same as for
minerals and rocks. However, good reference
specimens are often hard to come by other than
from commercial sources. Even from the latter,
the specimens may sometimes be fossil replicas
rather than the fossils themselves.

A piece of detective work (pp. 37,38)

The tracks (Figs. 79 & 81) suggest that the
trilobite had two claws on each leg. The two long
parallel grooves at the edges of each track
(Fig. 79) must have been made by the spines pro-
jecting down from its head (Fig. 80). The track
in part D of Fig. 81 was made as the trilobite
prepared for 'lift-off' (see Fig. 79).

How are fossils formed? (pp. 38-40)

Quick burial of dead creatures is much more likely
under water than on land, and this is a very
important reason why aquatic fossils are much
commoner than terrestial fossils.

*Activity 13 Making impressions and casts of shell
shells* (p. 39)

Each pupil or group requires a beaker or plastic
cup, a plastic spoon, a stick or a stirring rod, a
modern sea-shell, some plasticine or clay, some
petroleum jelly and access to some water. To get
a good cast, a shell with very well-marked, coarse
ribbing should be chosen.

Recognizing fossils (pp. 40-43)

In Fig. 83, fossils 1, 2, 5 and 7 are brachiopods
and fossils 3, 4, 6 and 8 are lamellibranchs.
Fig. 85 shows a lamellibranch shell with almost,
but not quite, brachiopod-type bilateral symmetry.

Activity 14 Using keys to identify some fossils
(p. 41)
Each pupil or group requires several unlabelled
fossil specimens (selected from those in Fig. 86)
and a hand lens.

Activity 15 Sorting out some lamellibranch shells
(p. 42)
Each pupil or group requires a selction of six
different fossil lamellibranchs (and possibly also
of ammonites), a ruler and a hand lens. Teachers
and pupils may also wish to consult a standard
reference book on fossils.

Fossils and time (pp. 43-45)

The exercise in Fig. 90 is based on one that first
appeared in the curriculum materials of the
Australian Science Education Project. The full
succession is:

$$R$$
$$A/S$$
$$B/T$$
$$C$$
$$D/J$$
$$K$$

There is a much more demanding correlation
exercise in Further study 3: MAKING A MATCH.

The length of geological time is very difficult to
make any sense of. The exercise on p. 45 is one
of several that can be used as an illustration.

Fossils and past climates (pp. 45,46)

The pollen evidence in Fig. 95 suggests that
around 120 000 years ago there was a warm period
sandwiched between two much colder periods.

STORIES IN THE ROCKS (pp. 47-64)

The emphasis in all these fieldwork case studies
is on the pupils acting as 'geological detectives'
in unravelling the evidence and piecing together

a geological 'story' for themselves. The case studies have been chosen to cover the provenance of a sedimentary deposit, the distinction between a lava flow and a sill, and the main geological structures - unconformities, folds and faults. Some of the later case studies (pp. 51-64) serve as an introduction to geological maps. It might be possible for the teacher to construct other case studies of a similar kind based on the school's local area or region: they could then be accompanied by rock specimens.

Ancient beach or ancient scree? (pp. 47,48)

The schist and shale pebbles shown in Fig. 97 are angular and obviously of very local origin. The more rounded quartz pebbles must have been carried from much further away to have suffered so much attrition. The shale pebbles are smaller than the schist pebbles because they are more easily worn down. The breccia must be post-Devonian because it contains pebbles of Devonian shale.

An igneous problem (or The Great Whin .... What? (pp. 48-51)

Fig. 100 shows well-marked vertical jointing but no bedding, and this suggests that the rock is igneous rather than sedimentary in origin. The molten material cooled more quickly close to the 'cold' sedimentary rocks below it (Fig. 101) so producing a 'chilled margin'. The slowest cooling must have occurred in the middle of the molten mass. The sedimentary rocks below the lower contact must be older than the dolerite because they have been 'baked' by it.

A sill is always younger than the sedimentary rocks both above and below it whereas a lava flow is younger than the rocks below it but older than the rocks on top of it (Fig. 103).

The evidence from the Lower Permian breccia (p. 50) suggests that the Great Whin Sill is pre-Permian in age. Since it is also post-Lower Carboniferous, its age must be between about 310 m.y. and 280 m.y. and this conclusion is in good agreement with its radiometric age. The dolerite of the Great Whin Sill is more resistant to weathering and erosion than the surrounding sedimentary rocks and so forms features like High Force, High Cup Nick and those shown in Figs. 105 and 106. It is also quarried for roadstone.

Fig. 107 shows that the Cleveland Dyke must be younger than the surrounding Jurassic shales which it has 'baked' and upturned. The dyke has a chilled margin close to both contacts.

Time-gaps (pp. 51-55)

The time-gap shown by the unconformity in Fig. 108) approximately spans the Devonian period, that is about 65 m.y.

Activity 16 Making a plasticine model of an unconformity (p. 52)

Each pupil or group requires some plasticine in two different colours, some strips of thin paper, a knife and a suitable flat working surface.

The teacher may prefer to demonstrate this activity to avoid the use of very large amounts of plasticine. During the time-gap represented by the unconformity, the Silurian rocks were tilted and uplifted above sea level, then eroded and finally submerged by the sea which deposited the horizontal layers of the Carboniferous limestone.

With care, the view in Fig. 114 can be matched with the west side of Ribblesdale on the map (Fig. 110). The large roadstone quarry in the Silurian rocks on the extreme left of Fig. 114 is the one about ½ kilometre west of the Ribble close to the southern edge of the map (Fig. 110). The large limestone quarry on the extreme right (with the prominent white scar and the factory) is the one about 1 kilometre west of Horton in Ribblesdale. The older rocks only outcrop where erosion has cut through the younger rock (the limestone) to form a deep valley.

In Fig. 116, the line of the unconformity cuts across the lines marking the contacts between the older Cambrian, Ordovician and Silurian rocks.

Folded rocks (pp. 56-60)

Fig. 121 shows that the Bargate Beds could not outcrop on the south side of the Tilling Bourne valley if they were to maintain the same northerly dip as on the north side. The fact that they are exposed between X and Y suggests that they, and the other rock formations, are folded into an anticline.

Activity 17 Making a plasticine model of an anticline (p. 58)

Each pupil or group requires some plasticine in three different colours, some strips of thin paper, a knife and a suitable flat working surface.

This activity represents the three stages in the formation of the Albury anticline - the deposition of the rock formations (starting with the Hythe Beds and ending with the Chalk), folding and uplift of them, and finally erosion to form the Tilling Bourne valley.

Broken rocks (pp. 60-64)

The successions in Fig. 127 are:

East side of fault	West side of fault
Oxford Clay	Calcareous Grit
Kellaways Sandstone	Oxford Clay
Middle Jurassic Sandstones	Kellaways Sandstone

Continued on page 16

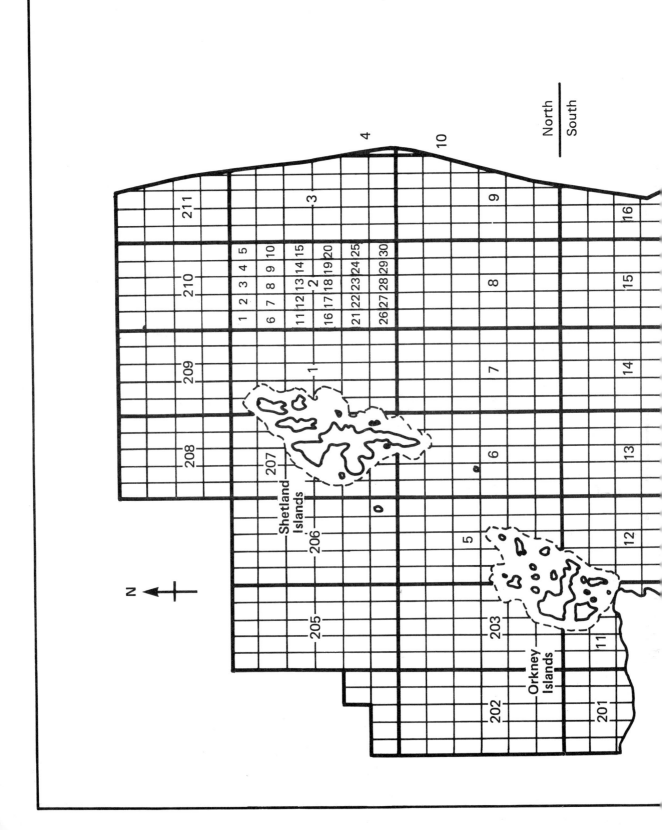

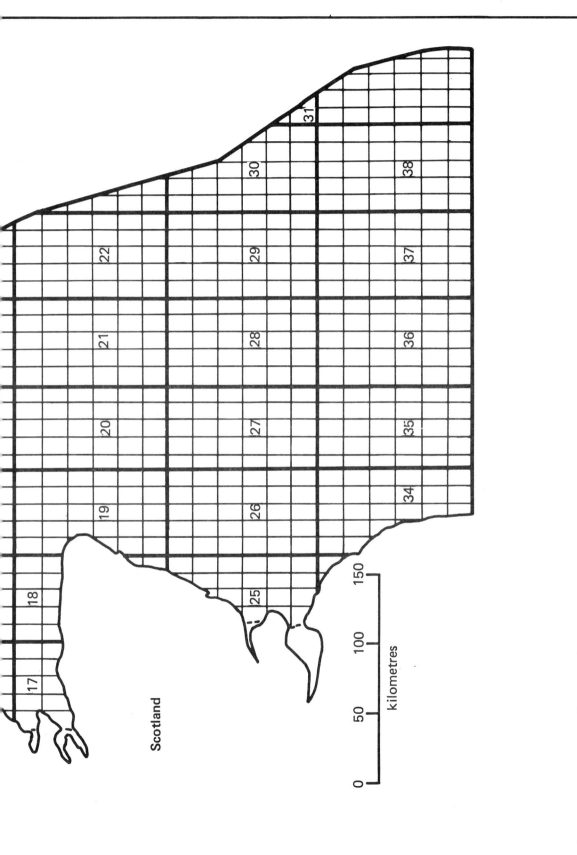

Find your own North Sea Oil
This map is for use in Further Study 6 of Book 4
(See page 22)

Continued from page 13

The throw of the fault shown in Fig. 127 is about
60 metres. In Fig. 128, the foreshore is rocky
because it is composed of the fairly resistant
Middle Jurassic Sandstones, not the less resistant
Oxford Clay or Kellaways Sandstone. The rocks
exposed in the Calf Allen Rocks are Middle
Jurassic Sandstones.

Activity 18 Making a plasticine model of a fault
(p. 61)
Each pupil or group requires some plasticine in
two different colours, a strip of thin paper, a
knife, a piece of wood or cardboard and a wood
block. The explanation for offset scarps caused
by a fault with a vertical displacement is not
easy, and this activity is best suited to able
pupils.

Fig. 131 showing the Peak fault at Ravenscar is
based on Fig. 10.11 in Michael Bradshaw's
The Earth : Past, Present and Future (Hodder &
Stoughton, 1980). The throw of this fault is
about 130 metres.

Further study 1: HOLES IN THE GROUND
(pp. 64-68)

The locations in Fig. 1.5 are as follows:

(A) Fig. 1.9   (B) Fig. 1.8   (C) Fig. 1.6
(D) Fig. 1.10   (E) Fig. 1.7

Further study 2:
THE BIRTH AND DEATH OF A VOLCANO
(pp. 68-71)

Fig. 2.4 shows that Surtsey grew northwards from
Surtur I as the southerly wind blew the ash in
that direction. The lava from Surtur II moved
southwards and so extended the island in the
opposite direction. From Fig. 2.7 it looks as if
more lava poured out of the vent in 1964 than in
1965.

Further study 3: MAKING A MATCH
(pp. 71-73)

This work could be linked to the account of the
Selby Coalfield in *Useful Materials from the
Earth,* the last book in the *Study the Earth*
series.

The Clay Cross Marine Band is missing in the
Kelfield and Whitemoor boreholes but the other
two marine bands and also the Low 'Estheria' Band
can be used for correlation purposes across all
three boreholes. The Barnsley seam is the
240-centimetre seam at 730 metres in the Kelfield
borehole, the 110-centimetre/100-centimetre split
seam at 590 metres in the Barlow borehole, and
the 210-centimetre seam at 875 metres in the
Whitemoor borehole.

Further study 4: PAST ENVIRONMENTS
(pp. 73-75)

This further study returns to the 'geological
detective' theme of using the present as the key
to the past. It is capable of considerable
extension in more advanced work, for example
along the lines of Section 6 of the Joint
Matriculation Board's Ordinary Level Syllabus in
Geology.

Further study 5: ROCK CYCLES IN THE PAST
(pp. 75-79)

This further study brings together mountain-
building (pp. 20-26), unconformities (pp. 51-55)
and radiometric ages for igneous rocks. It
could, along with an extension to Further study
4: PAST ENVIRONMENTS, provide a sound basis
for a more formal study of British stratigraphy.

The mountain-building at Oban (Fig. 5.1) probably
took place in the Ordovician period, at Siccar
Point (Fig. 5.2) in the Silurian or Devonian
period and at Llangollen (Fig. 5.3) in the
Devonian period. The radiometric ages in Fig. 5.4
are particularly grouped around 400 m.y. (at the
Silurian/Devonian boundary), 300 m.y. (close to
the Carboniferous/Permian boundary) and 60 m.y.
(close to the Cretaceous/Tertiary boundary). The
Oban unconformity cannot be linked to any of
these, but the Siccar Point and Llangollen
unconformities could be associated with the group
at 400 m.y. Also the Wells unconformity and the
Stock Hill fault (Figs. 5.5 and 5.6) could be
linked to the group at 300 m.y.

Because Fig. 5.9 shows vertical Eocene strata, it
can be concluded that the Alpine orogeny must have
been post-Eocene in age in England. So this event
cannot be closely associated with the date of the
igneous activity in western Scotland (Fig. 5.4).
Instead, the latter was caused by the initial
opening of the North Atlantic Ocean (Figs. 54 and
57).

Further study 6: GEOLOGY AND MOTORWAYS
(pp. 79, 80)

The route through the town centre (Figs. 6.2 and
6.3) would provide the best foundation but it
would clearly involve considerable demolition of
property. The coastal route would be longer,
would have major foundation problems and would
require a longer bridge. But it would avoid much
of the residential area. The route finally
chosen was the one nearest the hills, despite the
need to stabilize the areas of landslipped
material. This route is not much longer than the
town centre route and yet avoids most of the
built-up area.

USEFUL MATERIALS FROM THE EARTH

WHAT ARE THE EARTH'S RESOURCES? (pp. 3,4)

The cartoon strip (p. 2) could form the basis of a class discussion or a written exercise for pupils concerned with the main points on each side of the argument.

WATER - A RENEWABLE RESOURCE (pp. 5-14)

Water, water - everywhere? (pp. 5-7)

p. 6
Fig. 7 shows that many large towns and cities in eastern and southern England are situated a considerable distance from areas of relatively high rainfall where reservoirs can be established.

Water in rocks (pp. 7-11)

p. 8
Activity 1 should give porosity values of between 40% and 50% for loose materials. When using sand, it is important to allow sufficient time for the water to percolate through the sand before reading Z is taken.

p. 9
Activity 2 should give porosity values for rocks of up to 30%. The most suitable porous rocks are chalk or a friable Mesozoic sandstone.

Activity 4 How permeable are rocks? (p. 10)
The teacher will need to drill a hole about 10 mm long in each lump of rock. A hand drill is appropriate for friable sedimentary rocks but for most other rocks, a power drill must be used. The top of the hole should be slightly greater in diameter than the glass tube. A 100 mm length of glass tubing should be held upright in the hole and sealed in with silicone rubber 'bathtub caulk' available from D.I.Y. shops). This prevents any leakage of water upwards around the outside of the tube: the water can only move out of the hole by seeping through the rock itself.

Chalk or friable Mesozoic sandstones are suitable as examples of permeable rock; the water moves down the glass tube into these within a minute or two. Suitable impermeable rocks include shales and slates. In small lumps, limestones are usually impermeable, though they can be very permeable where they are criss-crossed with joints and bedding planes.

The plasticine plug shown in Fig. 13 is only necessary if pupils need convincing that the liquid level is not dropping due to the slow evaporation of the water.

The sets of apparatus can, of course, be stored and reused in other lessons. The shale specimens may, however, break along a bedding plane once they have become wet.

The distinction between porosity and permeability is a subtle one at this level but the practical work in *Activities 1-4* should help to make it clear.

Lake Vyrnwy (pp. 11-14)

p. 11
In *Activity 5* the level in the 'reservoir' rises or falls depending on the relative values of the inflow and the outflows. The 'flood' emphasizes that any reservoir has a maximum capacity and that it cannot store all the water when the inflow is exceptionally high.

p. 13
The drainage basin for the Vyrnwy has a much larger area than the drainage basin for the Conway - hence the choice of the Vyrnwy valley for the reservoir.

The summer inflow is about 210 million litres per day. So through the summer months the outflows generally exceed the inflow and the level of the reservoir drops. The winter inflow is about 490 million litres per day. So through the winter months the outflows generally do not exceed the inflow and the level of the reservoir rises. The reservoir is most likely to overflow its dam during winter storms or periods of rapid thaw of snow.

p. 14
The Vyrnwy dam (Fig. 21) was not built on the gravel because this would not have provided an impermeable seal for its base.

Figs. 22 and 23 provide a basis for a short class discussion about the issues surrounding the siting of large reservoirs in hilly areas. The Kielder reservoir in Northumberland is the most recent example.

TREES - A LIVING RESOURCE (pp. 15-19)

Using wood (pp. 15-17)

p. 15
Fig. 24 shows a large area of land, but the coniferous plantation on the lower hill slopes is approximately 5 ha.

The area of woodland needed to keep UK continuously supplied would be

$$300 \text{ km}^2 \text{ per annum for timber} \atop \times 80 \text{ for 80 year cycle} = 24\,000 \text{ km}^2$$

$$1\,000 \text{ km}^2 \text{ per annum for pulp} \atop \times 25 \text{ for 25 year cycle} = 25\,000 \text{ km}^2$$

Total requirement = 49 000 km²

The area of Wales = 20 000 km² approx.

Expanding a forest (pp. 17-19)

This section could be used as the basis of a decision-making simulation.

It is unlikely that some of the trees mentioned in Fig. 28 (e.g. Elm) would be planted today.

p. 19
Fig. 32 Area B has been planted.

ENERGY FROM THE EARTH (pp. 20-34)

Kinds of fuel (p. 20)

Fig. 33 has been adapted from an illustration in *Global Energy Resources* (BP Educational Service, Britannic House, Moor Lane, London. EC2Y 9BU).

Trapping oil and gas (pp. 21-23)

p. 21
In *Activity 6* water moves slowly up the lower lump of sandstone. It can cross into the upper lump at any point of contact between the two lumps. But the presence of an impermeable material (Fig. 35) prevents this.

p. 22
A suitable box for use in *Activity 7* is the one in which 'Tic-Tac' sweets are sold.

Looking for oil and gas (p. 23-26)

The BP Educational Service (see above) and the Shell Education Service (Shell UK Ltd., Shell-Mex House, Strand, London WC2) supply useful film-strips, wallcharts and booklets on the geological aspects of the oil industry.

p. 24
Semi-submersible rigs can be used in much deeper waters than jack-up rigs.

p. 25
The borehole in Fig. 42 would take about 29 days (i.e. a month) of continuous drilling to complete. If the 'good' days were spread evenly throughout the year, the drilling would actually take about 4 months. More realistically, the borehole could easily be finished within a summer period but

definitely could not be finished within a winter period.

p. 26
The borehole details in Fig. 44 were adapted from information provided in *Geology of the North-West European Continental Shelf Vol. 2, The North Sea* by R.M. Pegrum, G. Rees and D. Naylor (Graham Trotman and Dudley) 1975. They are, of course, simplified and generalized versions of much more complex geological successions. Possible reservoir rocks are the Jurassic sandstone in the top succession, the oldest Tertiary sands and the Jurassic sandstone in the middle succession, and the broken-up Permian limestone in the bottom succession.

Finding your own North Sea gas (pp. 27-30)

Much of the information in this section was obtained from Pegrum, Rees and Naylor's book (see above). This work is self-contained and could form the basis of an extended exercise in which pupils work systematically through the text.

Natural gas migrating upwards from the Coal Measures is likely to get trapped in the Lower Permian sandstone (Figs. 47, 49, 52 and 53). The cap rock is Permian rock salt. Another potential reservoir rock is the Triassic sandstone capped by rock salt (Figs. 49, 52 and 54). However, the gas can only migrate upwards from the Lower Permian sandstone if the whole succession is faulted. This condition is not fulfilled in the West Sole gasfield (Fig. 53), but in the Hewett gasfield (Fig. 54) gas has been able to move along the faults from the lower (Permian) reservoir to the higher (Triassic) reservoirs. In this latter case, gas was also able to migrate from the Permian sandstone to the lower Triassic sandstone via the permeable broken-up limestone.

Since the trend of the anticline and the faults in the West Sole gasfield is NW-SE (p. 29), it is sensible to look for more gas in the direction of the dotted arrows in Fig. 46(b). Hence pupils should suggest prospecting in the middle or the SE part of block 48, the SW corner of block 49, the extreme NE corner of block 47 or the extreme S of block 42.

Possible strikes of gas in these areas (mostly, as it happens, to the SE of West Sole) are:

```
47/3 ,  47/8   (Rough)
48/18,  48/21  (Important discovery boreholes)
48/29,  48/30,  52/5  (Hewett)
49/12,  49/17  (Viking)
49/16,  49/21  (Broken Bank)
49/17,  49/19,  49/23,  49/24  (Indefatigable)
49/26,  49/27,  53/2  (Leman)
```

Seams of coal (pp. 30,31)

The most suitable places for establishing a new coalfield in Fig. 55 are probably Coalville Common (opencast mining of the 250 cm seam) and Seaview (shaft mining of the 250 cm and 300 cm seams under the sea).

The Selby coalfield (pp. 31-34)

This work is self-contained and could form the basis of an extended exercise in which pupils work systematically from the text. An additional exercise on the Selby coalfield can be found in

Further study 3: MAKING A MATCH in *Rocks and Earth History*.

p. 33
The gradient of the Permian rocks (Fig. 62) is about 1 in 50 and the steeper gradient of the Barnsley seam is about 1 in 20. The Barnsley seam is 'cut out' (overstepped) west of Scalm Park by the Permian rocks, while east of Whitemoor the seam is at too great a depth for economic mining, at least for the present. The tunnels from Z to the Barnsley seam have a gradient of about 1 in 15 and are about 4 km long. It is useful that they do not have to pass through the Triassic sandstone because this is a very permeable rock and serious problems of water seepage would then have had to be tackled.

USING ROCKS (pp. 35-40)

Digging up limestone (pp. 37-39)

In *Activity 8* a very small lump of limestone weighing less than 20 g should be used along with about 200 cm^3 of bench dilute (2 M) hydrochloric acid.

Many limestones are of high grade and leave very little residue after treatment with dilute acid. The following data is taken from *Limestones* by F.J. North (Thomas Murby & Co., 1930) and gives an impression of the range of possibilities. The usual insoluble residues are sand and clay.

p. 39
A strong concrete can be made using a mixture of 3 parts limestone chippings, 2 parts sand and 1 part cement powder together with sufficient water to make a thick paste.

Limestone	Age	Locality	% CaCO$_3$	% MgCO$_3$	% Fe, Al$_2$O$_3$	% SiO$_2$, other insoluble residues
Grey Chalk	Cretaceous	Kent	94.09	0.31	1.29	3.61
Portland stone	Jurassic	Dorset	95.16	1.20	0.50	1.20
Great Oolite	Jurassic	Bath	94.52	2.50	-	1.20
Lias Limestone	Jurassic	Somerset	84.55	-	2.33	11.15
Pennine Limestone	Carboniferous	Derbyshire	98.90	0.45	0.25	0.75
Devonian Limestone	Devonian	Devon	94.00	0.80	3.30	1.90
Cornstone	Old Red Sandstone (Devonian)	Milford Haven	69.30	-	9.40	19.50
Wenlock Limestone	Silurian	Gwent	88.89	3.69	5.38	1.48
Precambrian Limestone	Precambrian	Anglesey	52.16	4.66	5.51	37.60

Stones for roads (p. 40)

A simple comparison of two sets of roadstone chippings (say limestone and dolerite chippings) can easily be devised. First an *impact* test could be used in which the number of 'standard' blows of a hammer required to break up a 'standard' chipping was counted. The smaller this number, the lower is the 'impact value' of the roadstone. Secondly an *attrition* test could be performed in which a fixed weight of chippings in a bag was moved about so that the chippings ground against one another for a fixed time, after which the new weight of the chippings (less the powder produced) could be found. The lower the loss in weight, the better is the roadstone's 'wear value'.

MINERALS AND METALS (pp. 41-48)

Forming ores (pp. 43-45)

Hot solutions, like ground water, move through very well jointed and faulted rocks but do not move so easily through less permeable rocks such as shales. Fig. 86 shows this directly; this conclusion can also be reached by studying the distribution of mineral veins in Fig. 85.

Getting the metal out of an ore (pp. 45-48)

p. 46
In *Activity 10* a suitable mixture is sand and

powdered galena (or powdered lead metal) in a ratio of about 5:1 by volume. Barite is the one gangue mineral in Fig. 90 that might possibly not get carried away from the bottom of the dish with the rest of these minerals.

Further study 1:
HOW PURE IS 'PURE' WATER?
(pp. 49-51)

p. 49
Activity 1.1 shows that dissolved calcium and magnesium compounds are the cause of hardness in water. Potassium and sodium compounds do not have this effect.

p. 50
Activity 1.2 shows that the carbonate hardness (caused by calcium hydrogencarbonate) can be removed by boiling the water. On the other hand, non-carbonate hardness (caused by calcium or magnesium sulphate) cannot be removed by boiling.

In Fig. 1.4, the softest water is from the Carboniferous gritstone (hardness grade 1); all the others have a hardness grade of 5. The water from the Triassic sandstone has the most non-carbonate hardness and this is because parts of the rock have a calcium sulphate 'cement' between the sand grains.

p. 51
The rocks in the hilly parts of England and Wales are old, impermeable rocks which are not weathered to produce many dissolved calcium and magnesium compounds.

Fig. 1.7 shows that the hardness grade of Severn water increases from just about 3 at Shrewsbury to 5 at Gloucester. Also the proportion of non-carbonate hardness increases the further downstream you go. This is because the Severn and also some of its tributaries flow over Triassic rocks which provide considerable amounts of dissolved calcium and magnesium compounds. One of the first of these tributaries meets the Severn just west of Shrewsbury. If the river had flowed over a lot of chalk or limestone rather than Triassic rocks, then the ratio of carbonate to non-carbonate hardness would have been far higher than it is in the Severn at Worcester and Gloucester.

Further study 2:
FARMERS AND THE EARTH'S RESOURCES
(pp. 52-61)

p. 52
This study suggests several ways of thinking about farming as an activity, and tries to present farming realistically.

Limits for farmers (p. 52)

Case study material could be used to expand this section, with examples of drainage, irrigation, shelter-belts, etc., and the choices of crops suitable for certain conditions. (*Air and Earth* in this series includes some relevant sections.)

Input and output (pp. 52-56)

Again case study material would be a useful supplement for this section.

p. 55
Fig. 2.5   A - 4 (the crops are growing);
           B - 5; C - 1; D - 3.
           (2 is not represented)

p. 56
Fig. 2.6   £ Sterling 1980

Natural cycles (pp. 56-59)

p. 56
Fig. 2.7   The information on the NPK bag label is printed below it.

p. 57
Line 5   The break in the cycle is made by removing the crop from the field.

Line 9   The N, P and K cycles could be 'repaired' by using the fertilizer in Fig. 2.7.

Line 10   For the N cycle the Nitrogen is important.
          For the P cycle the Phosphate is important.
          For the K cycle Potash is important.

Line 11   Phosphorus is contained in P_2O_3 and P_2O_5

Line 13   Potassium is contained in K_2O

p. 58
Line 10   Only 44% of the fertilizer is actually N, P and K.
          Some may be lost by wind and water erosion.

Line 19   With about 34 kg of nitrogen in a bag, he would need about 240 bags to replace the 8 000 kg used.

Line 31   The manufacturer suggests the equivalent of 1160 bags extra.

Line 34   Leaching, erosion, use by weeds etc. may remove some. At the same time the wheat crop may improve and use more than suggested in Fig. 2.8

Line 44   The 4 tonnes yield for cereals is the grain only.

p. 59
Lines   The answers to the questions depend on the
1 and 2   rotation chosen.

Line 3   Nitrogen would especially be needed for the potato crop.

Line 4   Calcium for the beans, but also possibly for the potatoes.

Food chains (pp. 59-60)

'Calories' in cookery and on diet sheets are each worth 1 000 calories. Fig. 2.11 in both cases the hectare is fertilized.

p. 60
One human needs 4 000 MJ, so

(i)   about $^4/50$ ha ($^1/12$ ha) under cereals

(ii)   about 2 ha used for grazing beef cattle

One human needs 20 kg protein, so

(i)   about $^2/25$ ha ($^1/12$ ha) under cereals

(ii)   about $^4/5$ ha used for grazing

Farming systems (pp. 60-61)

p. 61
Fig. 2.13

1 $\longrightarrow$ E $\longrightarrow$ (iii) [and just possibly (iv)]
2 $\longrightarrow$ C $\longrightarrow$ (ii)
3 $\longrightarrow$ A $\longrightarrow$ (vi)
4 $\longrightarrow$ B $\longrightarrow$ (v) [and just possibly (iv)]

Cause D does not fit any of the problems.

Remedy (i) does not remedy any of the problems.

Remedy (iv) is an alternative under special conditions only for 1 and in summer time for 4. In both cases the remedy is likely to prove too expensive anyway.

Further study 3: ROCKS FOR BUILDINGS
(pp. 62-64)

This further study should be supplemented, if possible, by fieldwork on building materials in the local village, town or city.

p. 62
South-East and East England are worst off for natural building stones.

p. 63
The wall in the foreground of Fig. 3.3 shows an increasing proportion of white limestone to the left and of darker gritstone to the right. The wall behind also shows the same changes.

p. 64
Limestone is weathered more quickly by polluted rain because of the latter's higher acidity.

Further study 4: BRICKS AND MORTAR
(pp. 65-69)

From clays to bricks   (pp. 65-68)

Activity 4.1 demonstrates the superior properties of fired bricks.

pp. 66-68
Many old bricks are orange or red in colour and this does not seem to have much to do with the colour of the original clay (Fig. 4.4), though iron-rich clays tend to give intensely red-coloured rather than orange or yellow bricks. However, the presence of a lot of calcium carbonate (chalk) in the clay has the effect of producing white or yellow bricks (Fig. 4.7).

From bricks to brick walls (pp. 68-69)

p. 68
In *Activity 4.2* the addition of water to the original chalk has no effect, but the addition of water to the powdered product of the experiment causes hissing and steaming and generates a considerable amount of heat. If only a little water is added during stage 2, the final product is a solid called slaked lime.

Further study 5: SEAS - ANCIENT AND MODERN
(pp. 70-75)

To follow this further study successfully, pupils will need an understanding of the underlying chemical principles.

p. 71
The reaction in which some marine animals extract calcium hydrogencarbonate from sea water to build their shells of calcium carbonate is represented by the following chemical equation:

$$Ca^{2+}(aq) + 2HCO_3^-(aq) \rightleftharpoons CaCO_3(s) + CO_2(aq) + H_2O(l)$$

Dissolved calcium   Solid
hydrogencarbonate   calcium
in sea water   carbonate

The reverse of this equation (from right to left) represents the reaction in which limestone is weathered (in this case, dissolved) to form calcium hydrogencarbonate.

p. 73
The order of solubility in water (Fig. 5.6) is:

potassium and
magnesium compounds
(most soluble)

sodium chloride

calcium sulphate

calcium carbonate
(least soluble)

p. 75
The halite and gypsum of the Midlands were formed by the repeated evaporation of landlocked, highly saline lakes situated in a desert.

The succession in Fig. 5.13 goes upwards from the limestone to anhydrite, then to halite and finally to a sylvite bed (mixed with some halite). This is the expected order. However, above the marl, there is more sylvite which merges upwards into a thick bed of halite; this is the reverse of what would be expected from Fig. 5.6.

Further study 6:
FIND YOUR OWN NORTH SEA OIL
(pp. 76-79)

The operation of this game is based on that developed by Rex Walford for his *North Sea Gas Game*.

It is very important that anyone running the game should previously have played through it themselves perhaps with a colleague.

OPERATIONAL ASPECTS

The teacher will need a map of the northern North Sea with blocks and sections marked on a scale of 1:1 500 000 but with no information provided about oil or gas finds (available from major oil companies - B.P., Shell etc.), a display surface for the map into which pins can be stuck, two kinds of large flat-headed pins with labels to represent Type A and Type B semi-submersible rigs (about 2 of Type A and 4 of Type B per 'company'), two colours of smaller round-headed pins (about 25 of one colour to represent oil or gas 'strikes' and 100 of another colour to represent unsuccessful 'drillings'), a set of 5 or 6 cards each in sealed envelopes with details of weather conditions for a round (see below), and the geological information provided below.

Each 'company' will need a copy of *Useful Materials from the Earth*, a duplicated copy of the company account sheet (Fig. 6.4) and of the company map (see pages 14-15), and, at the start of each round, the necessary information. For round 1, this information is given in the text (page 80); for rounds 2 and 3, it is provided below.

Companies

The class should be divided into five or six companies. Each company should have a card stating its name and starting capital. Rôles can be assigned to members of each company, someone with sound arithmetic should be in charge of the accounts.

Starting capital

Each company should start with £5 million. This allows them to buy only Type A drilling rigs and pay £1 million to bore, and have £1 million in reserve.
This is realistic since Type B rigs were not available at the start of exploration.

Weather cards

Each card simply states the weather in the Northern area and in the Southern area - the dividing line between 'North' and 'South' is marked on the company map. The weather in the North is worse than that in the South. Only five or six cards are necessary, one should have type 8 weather for the South and type 9 for the North. The rest should be 8 or below for both areas.

Briefing for the game

The briefing should include an introduction to the possible 'successions', an introduction to the map and its reference system, and an explanation, with an example, of keeping the balance sheet - this is the one difficult aspect of the game's operation.

PLAYING THE GAME

Points to note

(1) Make sure each rig pin has a reference number or name, and that companies carefully record the square in which they put rigs each round.

(2) If anyone explores in the far Northern area in the first round make sure that the weather card type 9 for the North is drawn! This is quite justified in the light of early 1970 experience, and will mean that Type A rigs in the North can't drill that round.

(3) Between rounds keep an account of borrowing from the 'Bank'. Companies often need encouragement between rounds 1 and 2, they can use several rigs at once if they want. The bank should be generous.

(4) A fourth round can be played, time permitting. By then everyone should be up in far northern waters and you should be sold out of rigs.

(5) The best way to deal with emergencies, new ideas, unexpected questions and so on is to ask yourself "What is likely to happen in real life?" and make a quick decision.

(6) The game is hectic for just one controller, and a sixth-form or senior assistant is very useful - perhaps to take charge of the map board, or to read out the results of drilling after each round.

Follow-up work on a map of North Sea oilfields is obviously appropriate, especially including a comparison of actual development with that of the simulation. This can lead to discussion of the rôle of geology, weather, capital, chance, distance etc. in the exploitation of resources.

The operation of the game should ensure that exploration and discovery broadly follow the actual sequence of events in 1969 and the early 1970s, that is, an initial concentration of activity in the southern blocks linked to the Cod and Ekofisk finds followed by a move into more northern waters in the light of very promising geological information, and the development of drilling rigs capable of functioning under more adverse weather conditions.

GEOLOGICAL ASPECTS

Information before round 2

Surveys have now shown that there are large faults at a depth of between 2 500 metres and 3 000 metres under the sea floor in blocks 3 and

9. The age of these faults is not yet known.

Oil has now been found in block 22.

Block and section	Reservoir rock	Depth in metres	Type of trap
22/17 and 22/18	Lower Tertiary sandstone in succession 5	2 500	Anticline with axis running NW-SE

Information before round 3

Surveys have now shown that the large faults at a depth of about 3 000 metres in blocks 3 and 9 can also be found in block 211. The faults are Jurassic in age.

Oil has now been found in three more blocks.

Block and section	Reservoir rock	Depth in metres	Type of trap
21/15, 22/11 22/12 (only traces so far)	Lower Tertiary sandstone in succession 6	2 000	Anticline with axis running NW-SE
3/4 (very large field)	Jurassic sandstone in succession 4	3 000	Fault running N-S
30/16	Broken-up Permian limestone in succession 7	2 500	Anticline with axis running NW-SE

No further information would be needed if a fourth round was attempted.

BOREHOLE INFORMATION FOR EACH BLOCK AND SECTION

Successions 1 to 8 and the information below obviously represent a very simplified version of North Sea geology. They are based on details in Pegrum R.M., Rees, G. and Naylor D., *Geology of the North-west European Continental Shelf,* (Graham Trotman Dudley, 1975), Vol. 2, *The North Sea* and they do not include any post-1974 developments.

For the 'companies', the directions of the anti-cline and fault axes are more helpful than the succession numbers. The former, when combined with the discovery of oil or gas traces, should help 'companies' to make 'strikes' during the following round. Successions 1 and 2 indicate that 'drillings' have been made on a geological platform where oil is unlikely to be found. The value of knowing something about the other successions is largely in the follow-up to the game when the teacher could provide a summary of the geology of the oilfields and gasfields in the northern half of the North Sea.

Successions

S 1-8   See Fig. 6.2 for details

Structures

Faults   (a) N-S faults in Jurassic rocks
         (b) NW-SE faults in Permian rocks

Anticlines   (c) N-S trending anticlines in Lower Tertiary rocks
             (d) NW-SE trending anticlines in Lower Tertiary rocks
             (e) NW-SE trending anticlines in Permian rocks

Faulted   (f) NW-SE trending anticlines in
anticlines   Jurassic rocks

N.B. The value (in millions of pounds) given for each 'strike' represents the annual income expected for each of the next ten years. The total value is therefore the annual value multiplied by ten.

209/3-5, 8-10, 14-15, 20		S1
210/1-2, 6-7, 11-13, 16-19, 21-30		S1
3-5, 8-10, 14-15, 20		S4
211/1-3, 6		S4
7	S4a Oil (trace)	
8-9		S4
11	S4a Oil (trace)	
12	S4a Oil (£30m)	
13-17	S4a Oil (trace)	
18	S4a Oil (£20m)	
19	S4a Oil (£10m)	
21	S4a Oil (£10m)	
22	S4a Oil (trace)	
23	S4a Oil (£20m)	
24	S4a Oil (£20m)	
25	S4a Oil (trace)	
26	S4a Oil (£10m)	
27	S4a Oil (£24m)	

28	S4a Oil (£24m)	16	S1
29	S4a Oil (£80m)	17	S4a Oil (£3m)
30	S4	18	S4a Oil (£3m)
2/1-4, 6-30	S1	19	S4
5	S4a Oil (£10m)	20	S5
4/25	S4a Gas (trace)	21	S1
30	S4	22-23	S4a Gas (trace)
3/1	S1	24	S5
2	S4a Oil (trace)	26	S1
3	S4a Oil (£30m)	27	S4a Gas (trace)
4	S4a Oil (£30m)	28	S4a Gas (£5m)
5	S4a Oil (£30m)	29	S5
6-7	S1	11/20, 23-30	S3
8	S4a Oil (£50m)	12/9-30	S3
9-10	S4a Oil (trace)	13/2-30	S3
11-12	S1	14/1	S6
13	S4	2-5	S1
14	S4a Oil (£10m)	6-8	S6
15	S4a Oil (£10m)	9-10	S1
16-18	S1	11-12	S6
19	S4a Gas (£5m)	13-15	S6f Oil (trace)
20	S4a Oil (trace)	16-18	S6
21-23	S1	19	S6f Oil (£10m)
24	S4a Gas (trace)	20	S6f Oil (£10m)
25	S4a Oil (£10m)	21-24	S6
26-28	S1	25	S6f Oil (trace)
29	S4a Gas (£5m)	26-30	S6
30	S4a Oil (trace)	15/1-5	S1
7/15, 19-20, 23-30	S1	6	S6f Oil (trace)
8/1-30	S1	7-10	S1
9/1-2	S1	11	S6f Oil (trace)
3	S4a Oil (trace)	12	S6f Oil (£10m)
4	S4a Gas (trace)	13-15	S1
5	S5	16	S6f Oil (£10m)
6	S1	17	S6f Oil (£30m)
7	S4a Oil (trace)	18	S6f Oil (trace)
8	S4a Oil (£10m)	19-20	S1
9	S4	21-23	S6f Oil (trace)
10	S5	24	S6f Oil (£10m)
11	S1	25	S6f Oil (trace)
12	S4a Oil (£7m)	26-28	S6
13	S4a Oil (£7m)	29-30	S6f Oil (trace)
14	S4	16/1-2	S1
15	S5	3	S4a Gas (trace)

4	S5
6-7	S1
8	S5
11-12	S1
13	S5
16-17	S1
18	S5
21-22	S6f Oil (trace)
23	S5
24	S5c Oil (trace)
26	S6f Oil (trace)
27	S6f Oil (£5m)
28	S6f Oil (£5m)
29	S5c Oil (£10m)
30	S5
17/1-11	S3
18/1-10	S3
19/1-10, 15	S3
13-14, 18-20, 23-25, 27-30	S2
20/1	S3
2-5	S6
6-7	S3
8-10	S6
11-12	S3
13-15	S6
16-18	S2
19-20	S8
21-30	S2
21/1	S6d Oil (£10m)
2-5	S6d (trace)
6	S6
7-8	S6d (trace)
9	S6d Oil (£20m)
10	S6d Oil (£60m)
11-14	S6
15	S6d Oil (trace)
15-25	S8
26-27	S2
28-30	S8
22/1-3	S6f Oil (trace)
4	S5c Oil (trace)
5	S5
6	S6d Oil (£20m)
7	S6

8-10	S5
11-12	S6d Oil (trace)
13-14	S5
15	S5d Gas (trace)
16	S5d Oil (trace)
17	S5d Oil (£12m)
18	S5d Oil (£12m)
19-20	S5d Oil (trace)
21-22	S8
23-25	S5d Oil (trace)
26-28	S8
29-30	S5d Oil (trace)
23/6, 11	S5
16	S5d Gas (£10m)
17	S5
21	S5d Oil (£10m)
22	S5d Gas (trace)
26-27	S5d Oil (trace)
26/2-15, 18-20, 24-25, 30	S2
27/1-30	S2
28/1-4. 6-24, 26-30	S2
5	S8
29/1-4	S8
5	S5
6-7	S2
8-10	S8
11-13	S2
14	S7
15	S7e Oil (trace)
16-30	S2
30/1	S5d Gas (trace)
2	S5d Gas (£6m)
3, 6	S5
7	S5d Gas (trace)
8	S5d Gas (£10m)
11-12	S7
13	S5d Oil (£10m)
14	S5d Oil (trace)
16	S7e Oil (£10m)
17	S7e Oil (trace)
18	S7b Oil (trace)
19	S5d Oil (trace)
20	S5